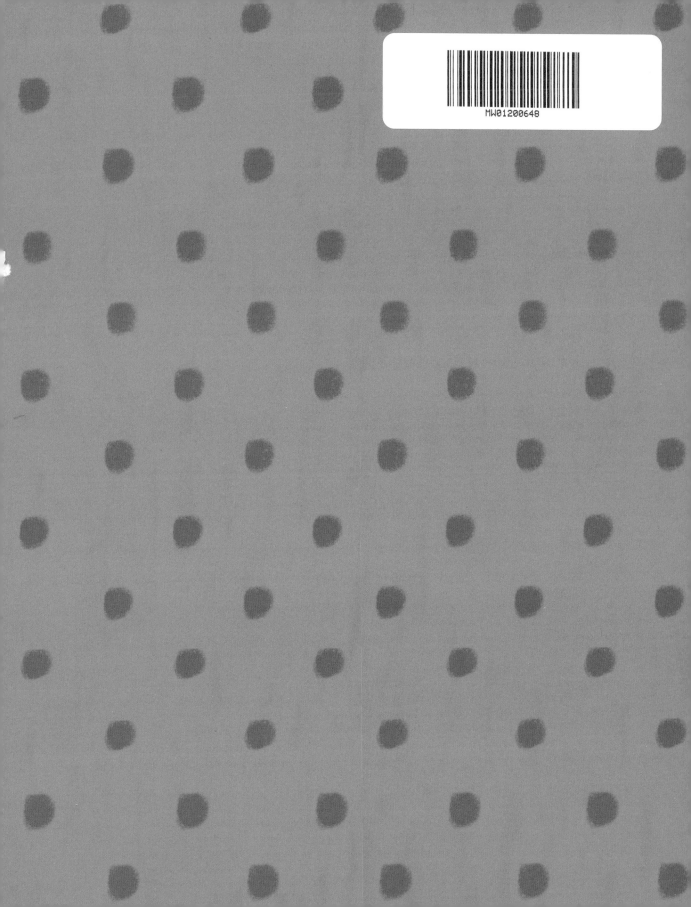

Little People, BIG DREAMS™
VIRGINIA WOOLF

Written by
Maria Isabel Sánchez Vegara

Illustrated by
Audrey Day

Frances Lincoln
Children's Books

Little Virginia was the youngest daughter of the Stephens, a family who lived in one of the nicest neighborhoods in London. Their home was often visited by artists and poets.

It was the perfect place for a girl who loved words!

Back then, it was rare for girls to be allowed to go to school, so Virginia and her sister Vanessa were taught at home by their parents. The lessons weren't very exciting. Still, they had a family library where Virginia spent long winters reading.

It was the summer she longed for most! Virginia spent her vacations in Cornwall, England, where she felt as free as a wave playing in the ocean. These happy memories would one day inspire some of her greatest books.

But great writers aren't made in a day! From the age of nine, Virginia wrote a weekly magazine about her family, full of lighthearted news. Sadly, it wasn't long before she had nothing but upsetting things to write about.

In nine years, she lost some of the people she loved most: her mom, her half-sister, and her dad. Virginia was so sad that sometimes she couldn't even do the things she used to enjoy.

She and her siblings decided that a different home would give them a fresh start.

In Bloomsbury, her new neighborhood, Virginia felt much better. Living with her closest siblings was fun, especially on Thursdays, when a group of thinkers and artists would come over to have interesting talks and share new ideas.

Virginia was publishing articles in newspapers and working on a novel, *The Voyage Out*, when a dear friend called Leonard Woolf proposed to her. They both shared a love for reading and writing, and he encouraged Virginia's work.

But just as she was finishing that first book, Virginia's mental health worsened and she had scary thoughts. This was something that happened to her a lot during her life. Leonard's love and care helped her through these dark times.

They created a peaceful home for her to work in, and started a company that printed most of her books, including *Mrs. Dalloway*.

It was the story of one day in a woman's life, written in such a new way that it made Virginia famous.

Instead of writing about big adventures, Virginia told everyday stories full of emotion. Her books showed readers what her characters were thinking and feeling. It was like being inside the characters' heads, seeing the world through their eyes!

Inspired by the love she had for her friend Vita, Virginia wrote *Orlando*, the beautiful story of a boy who grew up to become a woman.

Then she wrote a book about how girls, just like boys, needed their own space to create, and the freedom to chase their wildest dreams.

Unfortunately, her own dreams were ruined by a terrible war. Virginia was so worried about England being invaded that she couldn't focus on her writing. She felt as if she was being pulled deeper and deeper into sadness.

But by sharing her thoughts, feelings, and even worries with the world through her books, little Virginia taught us something wonderful:

when we open up about what's on our minds,
we realize we're not alone.

VIRGINIA WOOLF

(Born 1882 – Died 1941)

1902   1930

Virginia Stephen was born into a wealthy family in London. She was
one of eight children, which included siblings from her parents' previous
marriages. The family household was often full of artists and writers,
giving great inspiration to little Virginia. But when her mother, half-sister,
and father died just a few years apart, she was thrown into grief that made
her feel sad for a very long time. Virginia continued to feel deep sadness
often throughout her life. In 1904, she and her siblings, including her sister,
the painter Vanessa Bell, moved to a different neighborhood in London.
In their new home, they hosted a gathering of creative people, known as
the "Bloomsbury group," who met to share their art, writing, and ideas.
Before long, Virginia herself began writing books. She married a fellow

1939   2022

writer named Leonard, and changed her last name to Woolf. As well as
living in London, the couple had a house in the countryside, where Virginia
liked to write. She went on to create some of the most influential books
of all time, including *Mrs. Dalloway*, *To The Lighthouse,* and *Orlando*.
Her work was part of a cultural movement known as Modernism. It broke
free from the "normal" ways of doing things. For Virginia, that meant
writing about the thoughts, feelings, and memories of her characters—
something that had rarely been done before. And in her essays and
articles, she wrote about the barriers that held women back. Virginia left
behind treasured literature that has inspired generations of readers and
writers. Her life encourages us to be bold enough to try something new.

Want to read more?

Have a look at this great book:

Virginia Wolf by Kyo Maclear and Isabelle Arsenault

To my dear Wendy, for your endless imagination.

Text © 2025 Maria Isabel Sánchez Vegara. Illustrations © 2025 Audrey Day.
Original idea of the series by Maria Isabel Sánchez Vegara, published by Alba Editorial, S.L.U.
"Little People, BIG DREAMS" and "Pequeña & Grande" are trademarks of
Alba Editorial, S.L.U. and/or Beautifool Couple S.L.
First published in the US in 2025 by Frances Lincoln Children's Books, an imprint of The Quarto Group.
Quarto Boston North Shore, 100 Cummings Center, Suite 265D, Beverly, MA 01915, USA
Tel: +1 978-282-9590 **www.Quarto.com**
EEA Representation, WTS Tax d.o.o., Žanova ulica 3, 4000 Kranj, Slovenia.

This book is not authorized, licensed, or approved by the estate of Virginia Woolf.
Any faults are the publisher's who will be happy to rectify for future printings.
A CIP record for this book is available from the Library of Congress.
ISBN 978-1-83600-721-0
Set in Futura BT.

Published by Peter Marley · Managing editorial by Izzie Hewitt
Designed by Sasha Moxon, Izzy Bowman and Karissa Santos
Edited by Lucy Menzies
Production by Robin Boothroyd
Manufactured in Guangdong, China CC042025
1 3 5 7 9 8 6 4 2

Photographic acknowledgments (pages 28–29, from left to right): 1. Virginia Woolf, British author, 1902. (Photo by Fine Art Images/
Heritage Images/Getty Images.) 2. English novelist, critic, and essayist Virginia Woolf. (Photo by Hulton Archive/Getty Images.)
3. Portrait of English author Virginia Woolf as she sits cross-legged on a couch. London, England, 1939. (Photo by Gisele Freund/
Photo Researchers History/Getty Images.) 4. A statue of Virginia Woolf, which sits alongside the River Thames in Richmond,
on November 16, 2022, in London, England. The statue is the first life-size bronze artwork of Virginia Woolf,
created by acclaimed sculptor Laury Dizengremel. (Photo by Dan Kitwood/Getty Images.)

Collect the *Little People*, **BIG DREAMS**™ series:

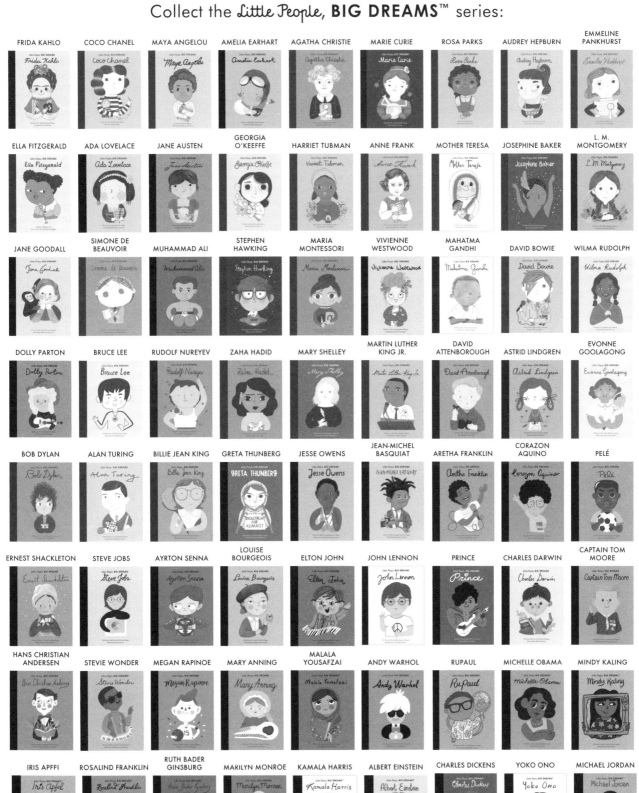

FRIDA KAHLO	COCO CHANEL	MAYA ANGELOU	AMELIA EARHART	AGATHA CHRISTIE	MARIE CURIE	ROSA PARKS	AUDREY HEPBURN	EMMELINE PANKHURST
ELLA FITZGERALD	ADA LOVELACE	JANE AUSTEN	GEORGIA O'KEEFFE	HARRIET TUBMAN	ANNE FRANK	MOTHER TERESA	JOSEPHINE BAKER	L. M. MONTGOMERY
JANE GOODALL	SIMONE DE BEAUVOIR	MUHAMMAD ALI	STEPHEN HAWKING	MARIA MONTESSORI	VIVIENNE WESTWOOD	MAHATMA GANDHI	DAVID BOWIE	WILMA RUDOLPH
DOLLY PARTON	BRUCE LEE	RUDOLF NUREYEV	ZAHA HADID	MARY SHELLEY	MARTIN LUTHER KING JR.	DAVID ATTENBOROUGH	ASTRID LINDGREN	EVONNE GOOLAGONG
BOB DYLAN	ALAN TURING	BILLIE JEAN KING	GRETA THUNBERG	JESSE OWENS	JEAN-MICHEL BASQUIAT	ARETHA FRANKLIN	CORAZON AQUINO	PELÉ
ERNEST SHACKLETON	STEVE JOBS	AYRTON SENNA	LOUISE BOURGEOIS	ELTON JOHN	JOHN LENNON	PRINCE	CHARLES DARWIN	CAPTAIN TOM MOORE
HANS CHRISTIAN ANDERSEN	STEVIE WONDER	MEGAN RAPINOE	MARY ANNING	MALALA YOUSAFZAI	ANDY WARHOL	RUPAUL	MICHELLE OBAMA	MINDY KALING
IRIS APFEL	ROSALIND FRANKLIN	RUTH BADER GINSBURG	MARILYN MONROE	KAMALA HARRIS	ALBERT EINSTEIN	CHARLES DICKENS	YOKO ONO	MICHAEL JORDAN

NELSON MANDELA PABLO PICASSO AMANDA GORMAN GLORIA STEINEM FLORENCE NIGHTINGALE HARRY HOUDINI J.R.R. TOLKIEN ELVIS PRESLEY NEIL ARMSTRONG

ALEXANDER VON HUMBOLDT NIKOLA TESLA WILMA MANKILLER MARCUS RASHFORD LAVERNE COX MAE JEMISON DWAYNE JOHNSON HELEN KELLER ANNA PAVLOVA

QUEEN ELIZABETH TERRY FOX HEDY LAMARR SHAKIRA FREDDIE MERCURY LEWIS HAMILTON LOUIS PASTEUR PRINCESS DIANA DAVID HOCKNEY

VANESSA NAKATE OLIVE MORRIS KING CHARLES MOZART STEVE IRWIN JÜRGEN KLOPP LEO MESSI SALLY RIDE TENZING NORGAY

KYLIE MINOGUE BEYONCÉ TAYLOR SWIFT RAFA NADAL USAIN BOLT SIMONE BILES STAN LEE LEONARD COHEN VINCENT VAN GOGH

MARY KOM SALVADOR DALÍ ANTOINE DE SAINT-EXUPÉRY DAVID BECKHAM KATHERINE JOHNSON PATRICK MAHOMES

YAYOI KUSAMA ROALD DAHL HARRY STYLES WILLIAM KAMKWAMBA MARY EARPS YVES SAINT LAURENT

BOB MARLEY VIRGINIA WOOLF

Scan the QR code for free activity sheets, teachers' notes and more information about the series at www.littlepeoplebigdreams.com